Mallards & Wood Ducks

Grace & Beauty on Water

Love of Nature Series

ISSUE 20

Dr. Richard A. NeSmith

Applied **P**rinciples of **E**ducation & *Learning*

APE-Learning

© **2020 Richard A. NeSmith**
Love of Nature Series

dr.nesmith@gmail.com

http://richardnesmith.obior.cc

All images in this book are copyright by their respective photographers.

Dr. Richard A. NeSmith
Winter Haven, FL 33884

July 2021

ISBN: 9798560500535

FLESCH-KINCAID GRADE LEVEL: 7.7

Mallards & Wood Ducks

Ducks are birds and are identified in the class called **Aves**. Of the more than 10,400 living species, ducks make up less than *two percent* of birds.[1] As a class, birds are warm-blooded vertebrates characterized by:

❶ feathers

❷ toothless beaked jaws

❸ hard-shelled eggs

❹ a high metabolic rate

❺ keen vision

❻ a four-chambered heart

❼ and a sturdy lightweight skeleton

The term **duck** comes from Old English "dūce," meaning

"diver," or to *bend down very low*. This name may be referring

---

[1] There are 180 species of ducks.

to a duck's habit of putting its head just underwater. Or that some ducks feed by diving deep underwater. Today, if someone yells at you to "duck," you quickly put your head down.

A more specific description of birds than Aves is *gamefowl*, *landfowl*, or *waterfowl*. Ducks, with their water attraction, of course, are *waterfowl*. Ducks are related to geese and swans, but the duck is the smallest of them all.[2] Ducks have shorter necks and wings than other waterfowl and have large bills and plump, stouter bodies.

The most common and most recognized species of duck is the Mallard or Wild duck. Wood Ducks are also very popular as they also have **iridescent** (*shimmering*) colors.

Overall, ducks are quite popular in the United States. Even comics and cartoons seem to be successful in humanizing[3] them for our entertainment, such as Walt Disney's Donald Duck and Warner Brothers' Daffy Duck. Then there is Howard the Duck, Darkwing Duck, Scrooge McDuck, Huey, Dewy, and Louie. Besides some of the gorgeous plumage colors many ducks have, maybe we are fond of ducks because of their funny and unique waddling walk.

Daffy Duck, a Looney Tunes/Merrie Melodies character created by Warner's Brothers (1937-1968).

---

[2] All from the taxonomic family **Anatidae** (Latin, meaning *duck*) which also includes swans and geese.

[3] Anthropomorphism – that of attributing human characteristics or behavior to an animal or object.

Range

Ducks are aquatic birds living in freshwater and seawater and found on every continent except Antarctica. And though some domestic ducks might not have a lovely pond to swim in, ducks do need to submerge their whole head underwater to keep their mucous membranes moist.

Most species of ducks migrate every year. They usually travel to warmer areas or where the water does not freeze. Ducks do not fare well on frozen ponds and lakes, so they typically

leave before that occurs. This migration enables them to breed and build a nest in a climate better suited for **brooding** (*hatching*) offspring. However, some hatch their young before a migration occurs. Some ducks migrate thousands of miles each year.

After a general overview of ducks, we will consider two common species of ducks: **Mallards** and **Wood Ducks**.

Characteristics

Male ducks are called **drakes,** and females are called **hens** or simply **ducks**. There is some evidence of slight differences in the sexes (**sexual dimorphism**), such as in the feathers' colors (**plumage**) and calls they make. The male's **molt** (*shed or lose old flight feathers so new ones can grow in their place*) twice a year. This event usually occurs at the end of the breeding season. Molting can leave them flightless, thus vulnerable, for three to four weeks. During such periods, they will become more elusive and secretive. With many hen ducks, it appears that the females only molt once annually, or the spring molt is so mild it is almost unnoticeable. Females lay large groups of eggs (called **clutches**) of smooth-shelled eggs. Both sexes have overlapping *scales* on the skin of the legs.

Ducks, generally, are divided into three major groups based on their characteristic behaviors:

1. **dabbling** (shallow water)

2. **diving** (deep water)

3. **perching** (tree nesting)

Diving ducks are heavier than those who do not dive. These can be **marine** (saltwater) or fresh, but the majority are marine. They swim around and then wholly dive underwater, feeding on the plants, fish, and small creatures living below the surface. They can swim underwater for a minute or longer before coming up for air. To take off and fly, the diving ducks need a runway because their wings are small and further back on their body. This design seems to be the best for diving.

Dabbling ducks, which include Mallards, feed on the water's surface, land, or *ducking* their head underwater. They are often seen feeding while swimming. Their beaks have a comb-like structure called a **pecten**. This helps the duck extract slippery food and filter nutrients out of the water like a strainer or sieve would do used in the kitchen.

Mallards and other dabbling ducks do not dive for food, but they often plunge their headfirst underwater with their tails sticking straight up. These ducks do not require a runway for flight as their wings are larger than the diving ducks and are more forward on their body, enabling them to do quick take-offs.

Perching ducks are regularly found resting in trees along wooded waterways and other areas with suitable nesting

trees. They may nest 10 or 12 feet above the ground. The Muscovy, **Wood**, and Mandarin ducks are examples of perching ducks. These ducks have modified feet with a rectangular **tarsal** (toe) scale pattern with **scutes**[4] above the middle toe base, providing them with a means of balancing on tree branches. Perching ducks are closely similar to dabbling ducks.

Ducks are **diurnal** (active during the daylight hours) and adapted for flying, swimming, floating, and in some cases, diving underwater. They have some unique characteristics separating them from most animals, particularly their feathers, webbed feet, and quacking.

---

[4] Scutes, meaning *shield* is a bony external plate or scale overlaid with horn a waterproof keratin protein. These are similar as those found on turtles, alligators, and armadillos.

Feathers

Feathers are the bird's outer covering and formed from a waterproof **keratin** protein along the duck's **epidermis** (the skin's outermost layer). They are complex, lightweight, and firm structures and only form from well-defined areas or tracks.

Feathers have a complicated microstructure, which truly makes it possible for the birds to fly. The base of a feather contains a **quill**. A quill is a smooth, long, hollow protein part of the feather with little or no coloration (or lightly whitish transparent). Quills were once used as writing pens up to the mid-19th century. The *quill pen's* hollow tube was dipped into an ink well, taking in ink. It was then quickly applied to paper.

Down feathers (down fibers) lie underneath the bird's larger protective feathers and develop from the same place as other feathers. These are light, soft, and fluffy and contain no

quills. Ducks have very waterproofed plumage due to the interlocking nature and the oily coating on the **feathers**. Down feathers are used in many products, such as padding for pillows and bed comforters.

Feathers enable birds and ducks to fly and stay warm (acting as ***thermal insulation***). It also helps them avoid getting wet even while floating in water since wet feathers cannot fly. Like birds, ducks pick up oil on their beaks by rubbing against the **preening gland** near their tail. They then rub it over the feathers. Spreading the oil coats and covers the feathers acting as a water barrier and insulates the small microscopic interlocking hooks called **barbs** (which possess additional branches called **barbules**).[5] These barbs interlock

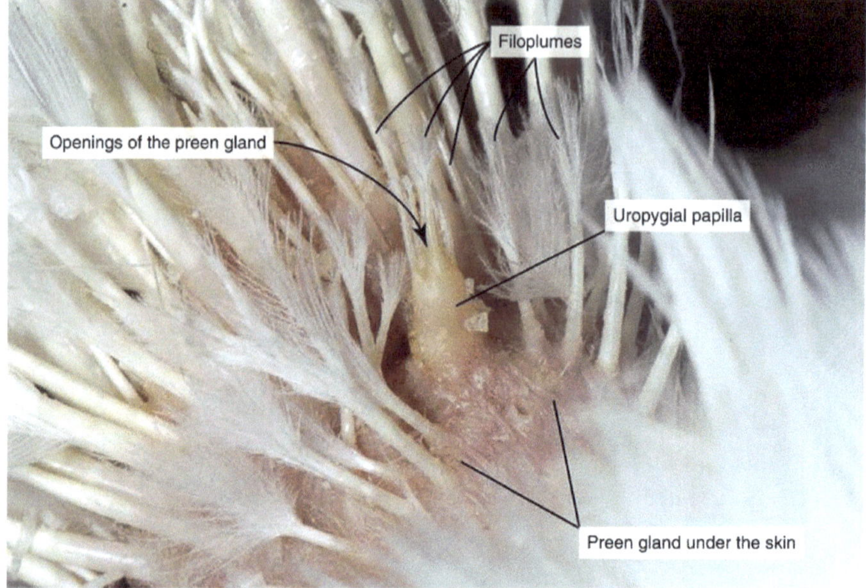

Uropygial/preening gland underneath the feathers. Source: https://bitchinchickens.com/2020/05/28/chicken-preening-uropygial-gland/#jp-carousel-7713

with one another, creating a smooth, flexible, and resilient surface that supports flight and sheds water. This fact explains the origin of the phrase, *like water on a duck's back*.

Ducks keep their feathers clean by *preening* and do this several times a day. This ritual is needed to ❶ prevent water

---

[5] Barbs grow from the central shaft called the rachis.

from penetrating through the feathers and ❷ to keep the

feathers soft and flexible.

You may have witnessed this if you have seen them putting their heads in awkward positions. It enables them to use their beaks to rejoin the tiny **barbs**. This practice is very similar to our reconnecting a Velcro™ strip or aligning and closing a Ziploc™ baggie. Having done that task, they then

reapply oil from the **uropygial gland**.[6]

There are ***six types of feathers*** on most birds.

1. **contour feathers** - give shape and color to the bird.

2. **flight feathers** - on the wings and tail.

3. **semiplume feathers** - a cross between *down* and *contour* feathers.

4. **downy feathers** - have little or no shaft and are soft and fluffy and help insulate birds by trapping air.

5. **filoplume feathers** - incredibly small feathers with tufts of barbs at the end of the shaft. These are attached to muscles for

---

[6] This oil or preening gland is not normally visible unless the feathers are parted in this area or the gland becomes infected or inflamed.

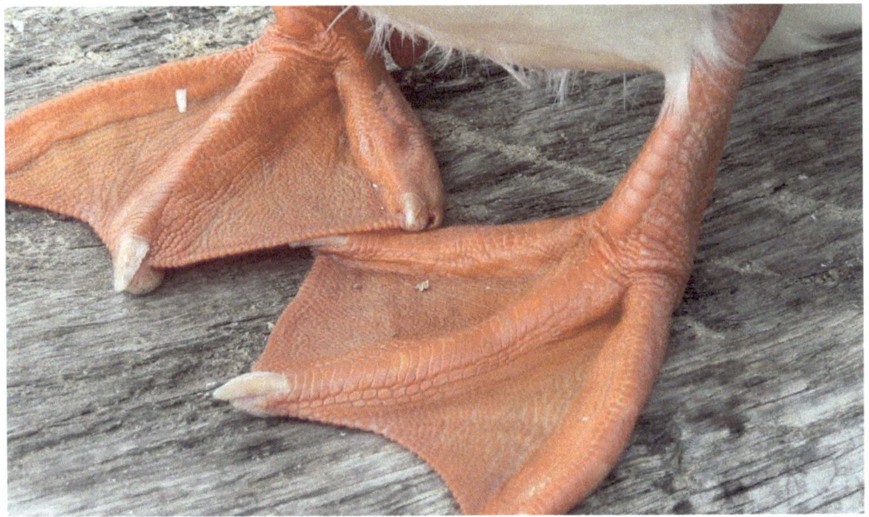

movement and connected to nerve endings.

⑥ **bristle feathers** - the simplest feathers, with a stiff rachis (the main feather shaft), usually lack barb branches. It is found at the base around the mouth and eyes acting like eyelashes protecting the duck's face.

Webbed-feet

Ducks have webbed feet, acting like paddles.[7] So, they are excellent swimmers, assisted by the fact that they are very **buoyant**.[8] In other words, they do not have to paddle to stay afloat, for their bodies are naturally stable in water. Because they weigh *less* than the water they displace, making them excellent at floating and swimming. The webbed feet, however, do make them waddle or shuffle as they walk. Waddling is caused by their taking short, clumsy steps, which causes them to swing unsteadily from side to side.

---

[7] The duck's feet are palmate or lobed with three webbed front toes and the hind toe (called the *hallux*) is small and elevated.

[8] Items float if the amount of water an object *displaces* is <u>less</u> than its amount of volume per mass (density). Density = mass/volume.

Though feathers act as insulation and help them maintain average body temperatures, so do a duck's feet. Their average body temperature is 107.5°F (41.9°C).[9] The temperature of the duck's feet, for example, could be just above freezing. But waterfowl have reduced volume (amount) of blood flow to their feet by *constricting* **blood vessels** in their legs. This process limits heat loss.

The cooled blood from a dabbling ducks' feet receives a small amount of cold blood returning to the legs veins. So,

---

[9] Younger ducklings can have a body temperature ranging between 102-106°F (38.9-41.1°C).

the blood is *rewarmed* back to body temperature as it passes into the returning veins. This mechanism ensures that 1) blood is warmed before it returns to the heart, reducing the chance of **hypothermia**, and 2) a reduction in nerves means that a duck's feet do not feel the cold, even if swimming in icy waters.

Quacking!

One fable about ducks is that their quack does not echo. This myth is false. Ducks communicate in many ways. Most ducks do **quack,** but each species of duck has its own unique, different quack. Even some male and female ducks in the same species each may have their specific kinds of quack. The **Wood Duck**, however, does not quack. They squeal.

For example, some quacking can be that of a female duck communicating just before laying her eggs. This sound could

be to warn other ducks of her claim of that nesting site.

The production of eggs is affected by daylight. As summer has longer days, *the more daylight will mean the more eggs laid.* Conversely, in months when daylight is shorter, ducks slow down their production of eggs and sometimes stop laying eggs altogether.

Later, while brooding (incubating) her eggs, she may be making herself known to her unhatched ducklings. This *quack talk* enables the duckling to recognize their mother's voice at **pipping**[10] and ensure they follow her lead. A duck's mouth, the bill, comes in different shapes, sizes, and colors and determines how the duck will hunt or forage for food.

Diet

Ducks are **omnivores** (eating plants and animals). They feed on aquatic plants such as grasses, sedges, water lily seeds, mangrove seeds, and tubers. In addition, they eat animals such as larvae and pupae found under rocks, insects and their grubs, worms, crustaceans, mollusks (snails and crabs), small fish, and reptiles. Because of potential dangers, ducks are well acquainted with *eat-and-run* (or fly) meals.

Ducks, and other waterfowls, have a unique digestive system involving many organs. As a result, each species' bill is designed for acquiring specific types of food. Some ducks have

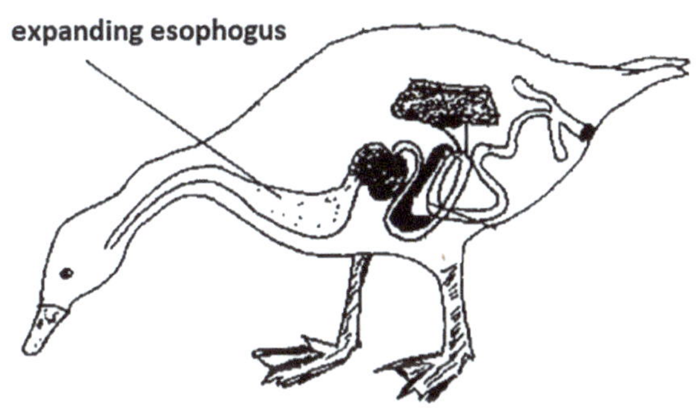

a **bill** intended for straining out tiny aquatic invertebrates. Wood Ducks, for example, have bills better equipped for picking up acorns and seeds from plants. Though ducks do not have teeth as we know them, a duck's bill can still produce a painful bite. A duck's bite can vary from just a slight pinch to a strong grab-and-pull, resulting in bruises.

---

[10] **Pipping** is when a chick or duckling is still in the egg and begins to crack the shell from the inside in order to break through the membrane and the world.

Mallard in molting season.

Though not quite as powerful, a duck bite can feel like being grabbed by a set of pliers gently pressed down. Some ducks, especially dominant drakes, can become very aggressive for any of three reasons: food, territory, or mates.

Though waterfowls do not have a real **crop**[11] like many birds, their **esophagus** (also called a **gullet**) is slightly out of place in the neck and not directly in line with the trachea as in most animals. As a result, it has an elastic-like characteristic permitting it to expand. This expansion capability allows ducks to carry considerably more food from foraging than otherwise.

---

[11] Some birds do have a crop, such as pigeons, chickens, hawks, and eagles. It is a thin, muscular-walled expanded portion of the alimentary tract just before the stomach used for the storage of food prior to digestion.

Ducks naturally distributed in the wild tend to benefit the environment, particularly ponds and lakes. Algae can overrun ponds during the spring bloom, and ducks love to eat algae. They also do not mind dining on frogs.

Most of us enjoy ducks, and many of us offer them food to encourage them to come to us and stay around. They like it, and it seems to work! Even ducks like an easy meal.

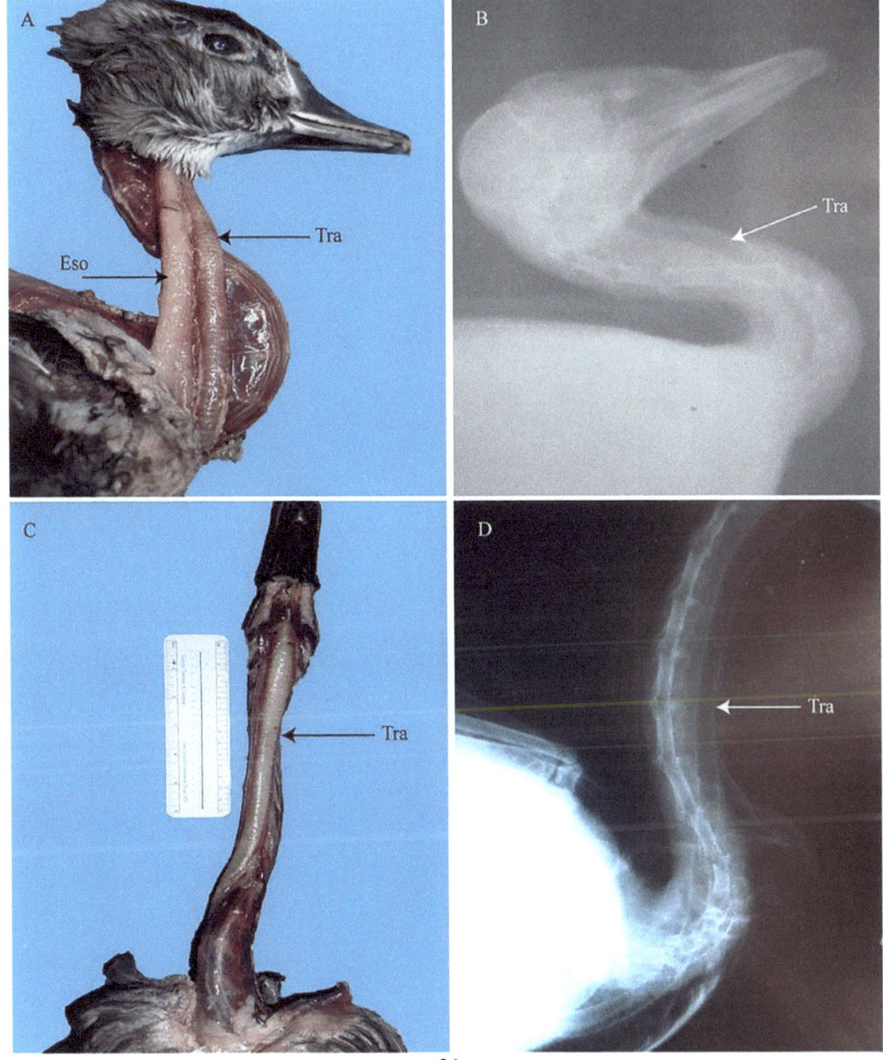

However, it is an inferior nutritional food source for them and not recommended. But the truth of the matter is that bread is *unsuitable* for ducks and often causes eventual health issues. Also, there may be local laws against feeding wild animals, including ducks. Better to ask before facing the consequences of a violation.

Besides health concerns, there is another reason for not feeding the ducks. It causes them and the geese to become *dependent on humans for food*. Humans feeding ducks can lead to their **starvation** and possibly death when the feedings stop. Ducks need to maintain their natural ability to forage and hunt for food themselves. Natural food sources are so much more healthier for them.

Gizzard

As food moves into a duck's stomach, the liver and pancreas

secrete digestive enzymes into the small intestine. Here the food is absorbed into the body. The food moves from the acid/enzyme bath to the **gizzard**.

Since ducks do not have teeth, they are unable to chew their food. Instead, the food swallowed by a duck is partially ground internally in their **gizzard**. The grinding is done by muscles and grit and small stones (**gastroliths**) moving the food substance around, much like a slow mixer. Friction reduces large substances into smaller ones. The gizzard's muscular wall and the gastroliths churn back and forth, *mechanically* breaking large food into smaller bits.

The gizzard has no digestive glands but has three main functions:

❶ As a filtration and absorption system where usable substances get moved into the bloodstream.

❷ It grinds up the swallowed food using the muscular wall and

swallowed gastroliths, and finally, as a holding tank.

Intestinal Tract

These softened pulverized nutrients leave the gizzard and are *chemically* broken by enzymes. In the **small intestines**, nutrients are absorbed across the intestinal lining. From there, they are taken by the bloodstream to every cell in the body. It is either stored or used to create glucose, which is eventually used to produce energy via mitochondria manufacturing energy (ATP).[12] On the way to the small intestines, nutrients are absorbed into the bloodstream. Waste continues and makes its way to the large intestines. Nutrients enter every cell in the body where it is used for cell growth or repair.

---

[12] ATP – Adenosine Triphosphate

Habitat

Ducks are usually found in places with water like oceans, marshes, rivers, ponds, and lakes. It is not uncommon to see them in local parks.[13] Being in and around water is necessary for ducks. First, they rely on water to maintain their

---

[13] Often mallards found in parks are crossbreeds and may be more difficult to identify due to missing some physical features or markings, such as lacking the white neck ring, may show white on the chest or be all dark. Or show oddly shaped crests on the head. Some hybrids look so different they may even be considered a separate species.

plumage, keep their eyes and nostrils moist and clean, and

remove **uric acid**[14] from their bodies. In comparison to other birds, ducks consume and excrete a lot of water. Ducks do not **urinate** (pee) because they do not have a **bladder** to hold their **urine**. Nor do they have a *urethra*, a tube where urine is typically released. Though ducks do not urinate, they produce a *pasty* white uric acid substance expelled in their feces (poop) mixture. This method of **excretion** is another reason why ducks require plenty of water to prevent kidney issues.

Behavior

Ducks are curious and friendly creatures and have been domesticated as pets and farm animals for more than 500 years. All *domesticated/farm* ducks are believed to be

---

[14] The common waste product found in urine.

descended from either the Mallards or the Muscovy ducks.

Ducks are very *social* creatures. They get along well with each other and seldom fight. If kept *solitary*, they will become unhappy and even depressed and lonely. They need and want to be in a *raft* or *paddling* of ducks.

Migration

Ducks **migrate** every year because of cold weather and food availability.[15] They cannot survive very cold weather, and as the weather changes, so do the amount of food available. So ducks migrate to milder climates for the winter. Warmer temperatures enable the ducks to stay healthy, continue

---

[15] Due to biological banding programs and neck collars, it has been found that ducks (and birds) will return year after year to the same wintering area.

foraging, or build nests to brood new ducklings.[16]

With this inborn genetic programming, called **instincts**[17], ducks determine when to leave a region and fly south to a warmer one. Some travel thousands of miles, often back to the same area from which they were first hatched. "Home" seems to be **instinctive** in the duck's mind, more so for the females than the males. Before summer, most migratory birds and ducks return to their original homes.

---

[16] Some ducks breeding grounds are actually in the north while others wait and breed in the warmer regions after migrating, so it is species-specific.

[17] Instincts are an innate (in-born), fixed patterns of behavior in animals in response to certain stimuli. Imprinting is a form of innate behavior. Instinctive behavior is often associated with survival. An example in ducks is *imprinting*.

Migration is a fascinating topic. Though still not fully understood, scientists believed some ducks navigate using the position of the sun and stars[18], polarized light[19], the magnetic north, and landforms like major rivers (such as the Mississippi River), coastlines, valleys, and even highways. Most birds likely use a combination of visual and nonvisual cues, as well as **homing**.[20]

Ducks tend to travel together in large **flocks**[21] along **routes** (called *flyways*)[22]. As a flock, the ducks fly in a V-shaped

---

[18] Use the stellar map as directional cues.

[19] It appears that some birds can use the *axes* of polarized light to determine the position of the sun and perform sun compass orientations. In one study, when magnets were placed on the heads of captive birds, they did not fly in the correct direction even on sunny days. This may be related to *homing*, the ability to find home when a bird is released in an unfamiliar place or from an unfamiliar direction, such as homing pigeons, however, little is known of this with ducks..

[20] Homing - An animal's ability to return to a place or territory after traveling a distance away from it.

[21] A group of ducks in the air are called a **flock**. A group on the ground are called a **raft** or **team** of ducks. A group of ducks on the water are called a **paddling of ducks**.

[22] The *Pacific Flyway* is an example of a major migratory bird highway, and the San Francisco Bay Area is one of the most important stopovers on the west coast. Such resting stops permit ducks to rest and feed before returning to their flight plan.

formation or pattern. The V-pattern is more aerodynamic and helps ducks reserve energy by taking turns in the front or nose, blocking the other ducks' wind. It is also a way that a flock can keep track of all the ducks in the group. This pattern works so well the United States Airforce fly their jets in the same V-shape formation because they found it to be more fuel-efficient.

Migration times and distances are not the same for all birds.

Ducks tend to begin their migration during the fall (August or September) and fly southwardly. Migratory ducks may travel at night, day, or even continuously. Some travel hundreds of miles while others thousands. Some may travel less than 100 miles. For some, migration is a slow, relaxed, almost a leisurely trip, but a swift and strenuous journey for

others. Ducks are strong fliers. Migrating flocks of Mallards have been estimated traveling at 55 miles per hour.

As one can imagine, those traveling long, strenuous journeys would have to have very powerful flight muscles and highly developed respiratory systems. Along with hollow bones, internal **air sacs**, and a streamlined body shape allow such birds to fly high, far, and fast for more extended periods and distance. Most migratory ducks and birds have to build up **fat reserves** to make such a journey. The rest-stops along the way enable them to sleep and feed before continuing. This rest is one crucial reason we have National Wildlife Refuges; to protect migratory birds and provide them with a non-threatened stopover. Such preserves need your support. Without them, many birds would perish.

Two of the **most common** ducks in North America include the Mallard ducks and the Wood Ducks.

Mallard (Anas *platyrhynchos*)

Mallards are typical *dabbling ducks* and are among the most popular, the easiest to identify, and the most hunted North American duck. The female Mallard makes loud honking quacks, whereas the male makes softer, rasping noises, which some say is not even a quack. Males also tend to whistle and utter lengthy nasal calls if disturbed, and similar aggressive calls directed at other males.

The wild Mallard is thought by some to be the ancestor of all domestic ducks. It has undergone numerous crossbreeding and mutations since domesticated (tamed) in China between 2,000 and 3,000 years ago. Mallards live in the Americas, Europe, Asia, North Africa and have been introduced to New Zealand and Australia.

The male Mallard has a glossy, almost fluorescent, green head, white ring around his neck, grey wings, and belly. The female's plumage is brown-speckled and blends in exceptionally well with the foliage. She also has a purple patch on her wing. Mallard ducks have a molting season, which makes them vulnerable since it stops them from flying.

Mallard pairs form long before the spring breeding season, often taking place in the autumn. But courtship can be seen to occur all winter. Mallard courtship will involve three or more males displaying the shaking of their heads and tails simultaneously, performing intricate bill dippings and bobbing movements, as well as whistling. Mating is led by the pair facing each other and repeatedly jerking their heads downward, a display called ***pumping***.

The drake also has an elaborate presentation to announce a successful mating. Immediately after **copulation**, he flings his head up and back and whistles. Then he swims around the female in a gesture called *nod-swimming* while she bathes. After mating, drakes lose their flight feathers, becoming flightless for several weeks.

Mallard pairs are usually **monogamous**, but paired males

pursue females other than their mates.[23] Only the female incubates the eggs and takes care of the ducklings. Mallards have been known to crossbreed, creating many various hybrid ducks.

The mating pair selects a nest site, most often in the early evening, with the female always in the lead. It may be located in fields, in tall grass, or on top of some mammal's lodge. It may take a week or more to select a site. The female constructs the nest from leaves, reeds, and grasses. During incubation, down feathers from the female's breast are added.

Two months after hatching, the **fledgling** period[24] has ended, and the duckling is now a **juvenile**. A juvenile can finally begin flying after three to four months of age. By that

---

[23] There are exceptions to the rule in what is called "extra-pair copulations." This is common among birds and in many species are consensual, but male Mallards often force these copulations, with several males chasing a single female and then mating with her.

[24] Period between hatching or birth and becoming capable of flight.

time, the wings are fully developed for flight (confirmed by the purple bright feathers' appearing on the Mallards).

Mallards live 5 to 10 years in the wild and 8+ years in captivity. The oldest known Mallard was a drake, a minimum of twenty-seven years, seven months old when shot in Arkansas in 2008. He had been banded in Louisiana in 1981.

Wood Duck (Aix *sponsa*)

The Wood Duck, sometimes called the Carolina Duck, is one of all North American most colorful and picturesque ducks. Wood Ducks are small colorful North American perching ducks and a popular game bird. They were once in danger of extinction due to overhunting and habitat destruction. Diligent conservation efforts have saved the species. Wood Ducks nest in tree cavities up to 50 feet (15 meters) off the ground. The construction of artificial nesting boxes, located on poles over and near water bodies, has been instrumental in halting the decline of breeding populations.

Both males and females have a characteristic head crest, a broad ridged comb, or tuft of feathers on top of the skull. It is absent in the summer plumage. Male Wood Ducks have two longitudinal white stripes with a purple and green head, red-brown breast flecked with white, and bronze sides are easily identifiable.

The female's unique feature is a white eye-ring; her body is a sooty dirty grey-brown, white throat, and white streaked

breast.

Wood Ducks breed across most central and eastern United

States, southeastern Canada, and along the Pacific coast from California to British Columbia. The nesting start varies according to location. In the Deep South, egg-laying can begin as early as late January, with many hens having more than one brood a season, ending in late summer.

Wood Duck pairs form strong lifelong bonds. They nest in trees no further than one mile from water. An average **clutch** of eggs contains about 12. Some build nests over water. Typically one egg is laid each day for 10 to 12 days.

In 28 to 30 days, the five to ten eggs or more in the clutch all hatch within two hours of one another, though laid over a two-week period. The chicks themselves synchronize their hatching,[25] signaling one another by clicks from within the

---

[25] Called *synchronous hatching.*

shell. Ducks are **precocial**.[26] A **duckling** is a young duck in *downy plumage*.

The next day they are ready to follow their mother. In those cases where nests were built over water, the ducklings simply jump out unharmed to make their way to water. The mother *hen* calls to her hatchlings but does not assist them in any way. As parents, both help raise and care for the offspring once they have hatched. Ducklings will forage and feast on aquatic insects and other small organisms. Adult woodies prefer acorns or nuts, depending on the habitat.

Upon hatching, many waterfowl are genetically programmed to recognize and follow movement of any kind. This natural event is called **imprinting**. Imprinting is a form of learning in which an animal gains its sense of *species identification*, not

---

[26] That is they are covered with down feathers and able to walk and leave the nest just a few hours after hatching

knowing what they are when they hatch. This event occurs during a critical period of development. It provides them with the species they will identify with for life and ensure their survival. Young birds will imprint on that which is in their presence at the time of the imprinting window. If that happens to be a human, dog, or cat, then that is what the duck will take on. Reversing the process is impossible. This is challenging for survival, for a human-imprinted duck has no fear of people. This lack of fear can sometimes lead to aggression toward humans.

The mother duck will keep her ducklings together to protect them from predators. Animals like hawks, snakes, raccoons, turtles, and even large fish will eat ducklings.

Most ducks breed and raise their young in the north, while *food* and *space* are abundant. Travel to warmer climates is closely linked to both of these factors. Ducks travel south to warmer climates during winter but return every summer to

their respective northern breeding grounds. Adult female ducks often return to former breeding sites. Sometimes Wood Ducks even return to the very same nest used the previous year.

Young ducks return to breeding areas at much lower rates than adult females, generally, because young ducks do not survive as well as adults.

Ducks are so cute and attractive, with such beautiful displays of colors. But, ducks can also cause health concerns. They can be carriers and transmitters of various disease-causing viruses and bacteria. One common problem is that of **bird flu**. Avian cholera, also called fowl cholera, caused by the bacterium Pasteurella *multocida*. It is a significant disease of domestic ducks. It is an exceptionally troublesome disease of ducks in some parts of Asia. This disease is associated with poor sanitation and standing water in duck pens. Also, ducks can expose people to salmonella bacteria, even if they look healthy and clean. People can be infected by coming in contact with bird droppings (**guano**). There are steps to avoid illness: Not handling ducks is the best way to prevent bird-related diseases. If one does handle a duck, then do not allow the duck to get close to the face, and, of course, washing hands thoroughly after handling one is always necessary.

Ducks are beautiful, graceful, and intriguing birds. Whether photographing in the wild, game-hunting from a boat or just watching them in the park, they seem to have a way of

endearing us to them. Try not to make ducks dependent on

you for food. They are wild animals and very well equipped to find the food they need to survive.

REVIEW

1. What two types of ducks are highlighted in this book?

2. Where are ducks not found, and why do you think they are not found there?

3. What are the three ways that ducks can be categorized?

4. Describe the plumage of the male and female Mallards? Why is the female coloration as it is?

5. What is a *dabbling* duck?

6. What is the purpose of down feathers, and how are they different from flight feathers?

7. Name two unique features about Wood Ducks?

8. How is a duck able to gather up a large amount of food?

9. What is imprinting? What would happen if you were tending to ducklings when they imprint?

10. Which duck is your favorite, and why is that so?

WOOD DUCKS

COLORING PAGE

http://www.supercoloring.com/pages/wood-duck-drake

Cat's Eyeview

Name:_______________________

Mallards & Wood Ducks: Grace & Beauty on Waterty and Grace

Carefully read each statement or clue. Write the correct letters in each box. Use the Word Bank if needed.

gullet   quack   dabbling   gizzard   social   energy   fledgling   down   mitochondria

daylight   whistle   diving   molting   keratin   perching   oil

Across

2. If it waddles, then it might ________.
5. Waterproof protein from which feathers are made.
8. These feathers keep the duck warm.
9. Creates energy in cells from food eaten
11. Heavier type of duck with smaller wings?
13. Ducks fly in V-formation because it saves ______.
14. These ducks nest in trees.
15. The female Mallard quacks, the male Mallard might ______.

Down

1. Another name for the esophagus'
3. Ready to fly!
4. Helps to break down large food particles.
6. Ducks do not like to be alone because they are very ______ creatures.
7. During this period, ducks are unable to fly and so more susceptible to predators.
8. Type of duck...bottoms up!
10. Used to keep the feathers (and the duck) dry
12. The production of eggs is affected by ______ hours.

INTERESTING SOURCES TO CONSIDER

1 Hour of Duck Sounds. Available at: https://youtu.be/I0IzyelQONI

10 Fun Facts About Ducks. Available at: https://youtu.be/zjvP3_DWK2I

10 Interesting Facts About Ducks. Available at:: https://youtu.be/rIeBjMBPheU

A Documentary About Ducks. Available at: https://youtu.be/DbewWSuL0lg

Amazing Mallard Duck Information. Available at: https://youtu.be/cwZJejen6ao

Brave Wood Ducklings Take 30-Foot Leap of Faith. Available at: https://youtu.be/IHl7N-Gj9QU

Commonly Encountered Ducks of Florida. UF/IFAS Extension Pinellas County Available at: https://youtu.be/WFeJQ5PAAuI

Deb & Stu Greenberg's Wood Duck Pond. Available at: https://youtu.be/5AyJuJlo0z4

Duck Facts for Kids. Available at: https://youtu.be/xIqs3NPe89E

Duck Facts. Available at: https://youtu.be/EcXcey4mohU

Duck: Animals For Kids. All Things Animal TV. Available at: https://youtu.be/ndiVL4plQDI

Mallard Duck - HD Mini-Documentary Available at: https://youtu.be/eHevNn-AVQg

The Mallard: Dabbling Duck – Observation. Available at: https://youtu.be/RxT80Z_MiWo

This is the Mallard. Available at: https://youtu.be/FOpW3Z9sVNg

ABOUT THE AUTHOR

Richard NeSmith is a native of Florida, USA. He grew up wading through the swamps of central Florida with his two younger brothers during the pre-Disney era, and unknowingly, falling in love with biology, wildlife, and nature. He has lived in seven American states, twice in Australia, and once in Mexico City. He holds eight university degrees and has taught for 14 years in secondary schools, here and abroad, and another 13 years as a professor in several American universities. His service includes professor of science education, Dean of Education, Campus Dean, and an online instructor. His passion for learning (and *how we learn*) did not develop until *after* graduating from high school. His only explanation for this is that *having a goal made all the difference in the world*. He enjoys reading, hiking, nature photography, golf, tennis, and RV camping.

http://richardnesmith.obior.cc

Applied **P**rinciples of **E**ducation & Learning *presents*

APE-Learning

AMAZON AUTHOR's PAGE:

https://www.amazon.com/author/richardnesmith

Educational, wildlife, and naturalist books
Dr. Richard NeSmith.

Issue 1
Raccoons:
Friendly Bandits
Dr. Richard NeSmith

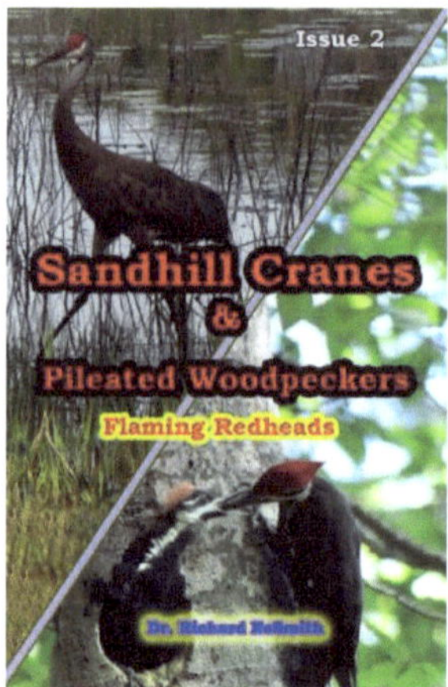
Issue 2
Sandhill Cranes
&
Pileated Woodpeckers
Flaming Redheads
Dr. Richard NeSmith

Issue 3
American
Alligators
&
Crocodiles
Dr. Richard NeSmith

Issue 4
Bobcats:
Ghostly Elusive
Dr. Richard NeSmith

Issue 5
Foxes:
Sneaky Rascals
Dr. Richard NeSmith

Issue 6
Armadillo:
Little Armored One
Dr. Richard NeSmith

Issue 7
Squirrels:
Bushy Tail Scampers
Dr. Richard NeSmith

Issue 8
River Otters:
Aquatic Clowns !
Dr. Richard NeSmith

Issue 9
Beavers:
Nature's Engineers !
Dr. Richard NeSmith

Issue 10
Black Bears
Titans of the Forest
Dr. Richard NeSmith

Issue 11
Freshwater
Turtles
Dr. Richard NeSmith

Issue 12
FUNGI, LICHENS
& MUSHROOMS
Dr. Richard NeSmith

Paperbacks: http://amazon.com/author/richardnesmith

e-books: https://bit.ly/3iuCgB3

---

[i] **Special thanks to the following who kindly provided permission to use their photographs.**

From Unsplash: bro-s-media, Andrea Lightfoot, Felix Hoffmann, Ana Karla-Parra, Amanda Swanepoel, Marc Pascual, Chandler Cruttenden, Anchor Lee, Brian Taylor, Artem Labunsky, Dave Willhite, Elisabeth N, Beanca du-Toit, Charles Chen, Dennis Buchner, Charles Jackson, Andrea Lightfoot,

From Pixabay: Ally White, Nile, Candid Shots, Rick Tremblay, Ikbeach, *and the prolific* skeeze.

Also, special thanks to **Stacey Diamond**, **Greg Jowers**, **Dr. Laurie Aleixo**, **Cathy Clements**, **Jackie Dibert**, **Raevyn Kay**, for their graciously sharing of some picturesque photographs of these beautiful creatures.

Special thanks to **Springerlink** for use of the uropygial gland photo.

Thank you, everyone.

Love Learning – Love Nature – Love Life